Sifting

SIFTING

Pearls From My Inner World

MEGHAN SALETTA

Published by Wisteria House Press, Chicago, IL
ISBN 9798218099329

Cover & Author Photo by Kim Carrier
Illustrations by Michelle Schultz
www.michelleschultzstudio.com

Edited and designed by Tell Tell Poetry

Printed in the United States of America

First Printing, 2022

Dedicated to the ones who have seen the full spectrum of my emotional landscape and loved me more for it — you have offered me permission to embrace all that I am + all that I feel.

"What is most personal is most universal"
-unknown

CONTENTS

ON THE WRITING PROCESS:

In August of 2017, I moved from the San Francisco Bay Area back to my hometown of Chicago to rest, reset and rebuild my life.

I had just ended a 7-year relationship with my boyfriend, was grieving the slow and painful loss of 2 beloved grandparents, and had my priorities shaken up as I watched my brother recover from severe burns following an apartment fire.

I had a lot of processing to do – a lot to sort out and a lot to heal. I craved quiet and space, so I rented a studio apartment in Logan Square and committed to giving myself this grace: an indefinite period of time where I would slow down and prioritize whatever felt good and natural to me in each moment. I was hungry to reconnect with myself on a soul level; to honor how I truly felt and what I truly needed; to build an authentic adult life; and to discover who I was independent of others' expectations of me.

From the stillness and space came these words, arriving like lovely, unexpected exhales on the El train, on early morning buses, on planes, and in quiet moments in my studio. Some I rushed to the nearest bathroom to write down. A few I wrote on the beaches of Maui while visiting an old friend. Some bubbled up after one too many margaritas at the Lonesome Rose. But each time a pearl of introspection came, I knew it was important. I knew it was sacred. I knew it was a message from my soul as it *sifted* through the sea of content I had fed it in my twenties.

After 3 years of living alone, being with myself, and having more fun than I ever imagined in Chicago, I felt so much lighter - and the spontaneous poems and words stopped coming. That's when I knew that I had healed what I needed to heal and it was time to organize them into the book you now hold in your hands.

My inner processing fell into a handful of categories which became the sections of this book:

Introspection (in the dark)

Love Me Wild (romantic relationships)

Wisdom + Encouragement

Creative Life

Introspection (in the light)

My deepest hope is that my words resonate with parts of your innermost self and journey; and that sharing my inner world with you inspires a deeper delving into your own. For there is nothing more freeing than embracing every part of ourselves; even the darkest of corners.

no matter where I go
or who I go with
I will always remain
Mine

Sifting

INTROSPECTION
(IN THE DARK)

Who are you
under *alllll* those layers
of conditioning?

I come from a culture
That worships the sun
We pretend we're OK
To warm everyone

I can be an anchor
& a feather
but never
at the same time

-dark v light

SIFTING

I am like a flower
I need nurturing
Watering & attention
The right soil and I bloom –
Face towards the sun
The wrong soil
And I wilt

-garden soul

Because I am female
You expect me always
To be sunshine
Warming you with
My words
My positivity
My compliance
My light
But you see
I am not always sunshine
Some days
I am as dark and angry
As a thunderstorm
As sad and lonely
As a birch tree in winter
As dizzying in my emotions
As a hurricane
Some days
I wake up and think
I might just deserve
To be whatever
I damn well please

-f e m a l e

SIFTING

I work
So that my soul can have a life
Without weight on her shoulders

Unburdened
By responsibility
Or striving

I protect her wild innocence
The way a mother protects
Her wide-eyed child

I remind her she has nothing to prove
I will never ask her to provide for me financially

She is an exhale
In a world of white knuckles

She is the untouchable magic
That we are all so desperate for

-muse

my coworker
is also an artist
we work on the 18th floor
of an office building
coated in shiny cold steel
like the armor we wear
to protect our souls
when we enter it.
sometimes
we keep our voices down
& talk feverishly about our dreams
sparks shooting from our tongues
eyes teeming with imagination
connected in deep knowing
that the job will be temporary
but our dreams are just waking up.

-day job

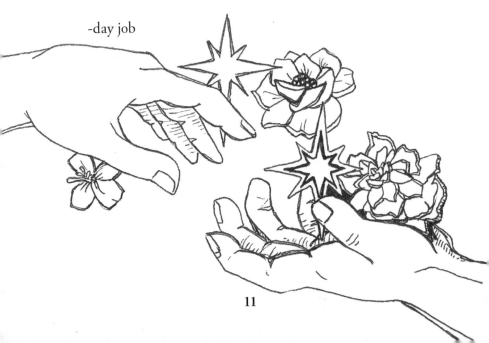

SIFTING

I haven't slept through the night in a long time
This aching emptiness keeps me up
Static in my gut
White noise that won't quit
I cannot settle into myself
My insides churn and twist
I am on guard where I once was at peace
A week of compliance and a weekend of anxiety
Resting with no release
Waiting to get on with it

-corporate confession

it's OK if I lose my job
it's not OK if I lose myself

SIFTING

not a brand
or a type
or a title
or a role
I'm
A
Soul

is it wrong
to want to use
the entirety of my time on earth
exclusively
in the arms of
beauty
love
&
pleasure
?

SIFTING

I constantly feel split
Between
The shiny positive persona I project
&
The deep, artistic processor I am

-I n t e g r a t e

Even with the door shut
It still feels like
I can never be alone enough

-introvert

SIFTING

Whenever I feel empty

It's because I haven't been filling

My own cup.

If I haven't been creating –

I've been stagnating.

If I haven't been sharing –

I've been hiding.

If I haven't been dreaming –

I haven't been living...

I've been

Surviving.

If I step into the light
And allow my true self
To be seen
My greatest fear
Is that I will lose the audience
I've built with my mask

What will happen
When the armor drops
And I stop trying to fit in
Or be 'understandable'
To those around me?

SIFTING

I have never felt more depressed
Than when I stopped allowing myself
Permission to feel the full spectrum
Of my emotions

I don't wanna drown with the cynics
I wanna rise with the hopeful

SIFTING

I am
Exhausted by consumerism
And watching those around me
Be consumed by it

Using it to numb
Using it in the place of
Honesty
Intimacy
Peace

Comfort has only ever really
Hurt me
Too much of it
Makes me into a lazy life
With little ambition
Little urgency
Little sense of purpose
It drains the color
From my sky
It leaves me
Stuck
It sucks me
Dry

MEGHAN SALETTA

Do you care what I think?
Do you know that I *mind*
When you blow past my words
And leave me behind?

Don't tell me I'm pretty
Then laugh at his jokes
Ignoring my brain
Is what hurts me the most

-patriarchy

SIFTING

when my mother calls and the conversation feels the same:
because *I* am not changing, *I* am not growing & *I* am
   deeply bored by my own life

-sleepwalker

movement is my drug
it tricks my mind into believing
that I am going somewhere
even if I am only
running in place
trying to forget

-endorphin escapist

SIFTING

when did I make it my job
to protect the whole world
from my authentic emotional expression?

-I can't even cry in front of my therapist

It's hard to feel fully
In a culture that doesn't really permit it
We aren't taught what to do with these
Big intense emotions
How to let them exist
How to let them move through us
Without believing something needs to be fixed
Or that something is wrong with us

-culture chains

SIFTING

I get angry
At pain
So it doesn't consume me
Lash out at the ones
Who are most like me
If you remind me of what hurts
Then you'll have to leave

I should have asked,
"Are you OK?"

I guess I didn't want to know.

I thought I couldn't take it if
The answer was, "No."

SIFTING

I haven't let myself go
Below the surface in a while
I'm terrified of what I'll find

-denial

there is a fine line
between solitude and loneliness
for it is lovely to be alone by choice
and devastating
to be alone by default

-the difference

SIFTING

My misery
Does NOT
Love company

MY misery
Longs for lightheartedness
Is desperate for laughter
And release

MY misery
Wants to escape itself
So it can be
At peace

I may have social anxiety
But I can always come home to me

SIFTING

when we laugh off
language that attacks
or belittles
wounds
or tears down
we permit
suffering + injustice
we allow shame to fester
+ sit as a dinner guest
at a table once holy

-speak up

When I stop feeling
I stop breathing
I start running
I start leaving

Insides burning
Clawing at the walls of my body
I want out

A different city
A different life
A different me

-runner

SIFTING

Please don't feel sorry for me when I spend time alone—
it is my saving grace.

There is nothing lonelier than being who you suspect
        everyone around you wants you to be
without ever knowing or nourishing your true self.

why
is it so much easier
to trust a complete stranger
than the beating of my own heart?

-self betrayal

SIFTING

no substance
on this earth
has ever done to me
what praise
has done to me

-people-pleaser

LOVE ME WILD

The Falling

The Breaking

On My Own

Rebound Season

Closure

THE FALLING

I remember
How free I felt
How the life
Came back to my limbs
And light flooded my body
I remember thinking
YES
This is how a heart should feel
This is how a soul should breathe
This is how to live a life

- soulmate

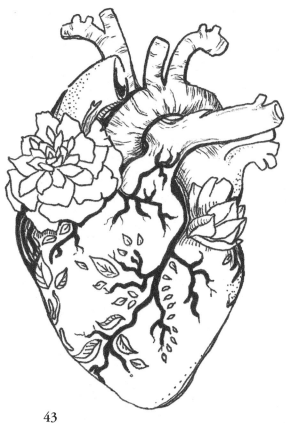

SIFTING

Yours was the first heart
That gave me rest

I knew when I met you
Your mind was a country
Your eyes held a lifetime
Your heart was the sea

I broke like a promise
I couldn't contain it
Fell with abandon
Into you and me

SIFTING

eyes full of stars
you give yourself away so easily

-innocent

a swimming pool of all my fears
still you wade through all my tears

SIFTING

In a world that loves to cover up
& hide away what's real
You gave me
Permission to feel

you have a heart
the size of
a universe

SIFTING

even in the dark
your eyes sparkle
even in pain
your heart glows

-magic man

most things in life
are temporary
I hope our love
Is not

SIFTING

you're patient when I'm restless
steady as I break
a heavy dose of heaven
a shot I'm glad to take

you're the answer to the question
the first light when I wake
a living breathing angel
& my heart could never fake

loving you

it's a letting go
it's a you-just-know
beyond all understanding

love is a fire
love is a flood
love is a soft landing

SIFTING

found a universe
in your eyes
open roads
open skies

swore you were
an angel from above
there's nothing like
your first love

MEGHAN SALETTA

I was your something sunny
You were my something real

THE BREAKING

it was hard to hold your pain
'cause it fell on me like rain
& reminded me we're all the same

SIFTING

I don't exist to please you
I love but I don't need you

won't make myself smaller
or more understandable
or show up in doses
i know you can handle

SIFTING

Non-negotiable:

I have to be able to relax in my home environment
Without feeling like I am walking on eggshells

I love you most
When you appeal
To my sadness
And offer your support

But I worry
That suffering is all we share
That pity and comfort
Have become too routine

That we know how to wallow
But not how to rise
And most days,
I long to soar

the life we're chasing
is not 'happy ever after'
it's 'perfect 'til we shatter'

-toxic

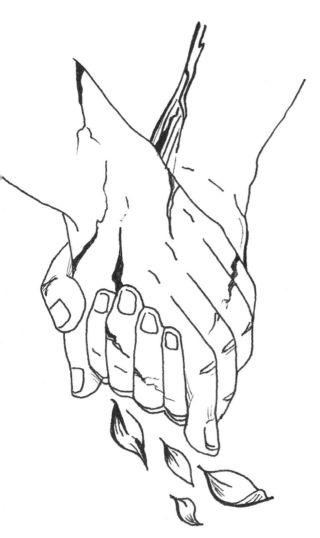

can't put me in a cage
expect me not to scream
rattle the bars
and call off the whole thing

- prisoner

SIFTING

our love is muddy
with the pain of
other things

how do I know
if I love you
or just want to
rescue you
from it all?

I think I lost my inner voice
It used to be so loud + clear
But now it seems I have no choice
About the way things go 'round here

SIFTING

The dance between us
Needs to feel different
We should be
Elevating each other
With our movements
Instead of dragging
Each other
　　Down

this love
is never at ease
& my mind
is never at peace
as long as you're sleeping
next to me

-e n d i n g s

SIFTING

I was already drowning
When you took away my life rafts

Whimsy was my drug
And you called for my sobriety

My colors could not conform
To the life in lines you drew for us

You wanted rules
And my soul wanted
Wildness

-mismatch

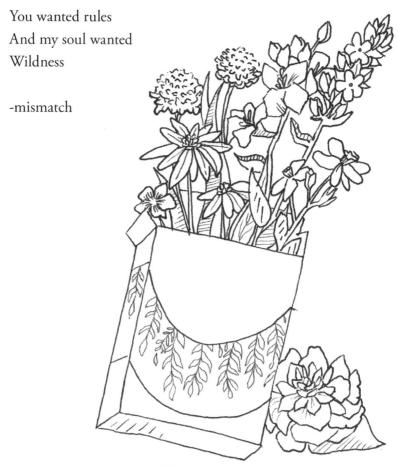

I've been holding my tongue
Biding my time
Playing out options + roads in my mind
Reminding myself
It's OK to cut ties
And start over

SIFTING

she got to a certain point
and realized
if she didn't leave now
she would lose every
magic, tender, unique thing about herself

-awakening

if it clips your wings
if it drags you down
don't keep it around

-weight

my soul was a desert
you didn't want me to water it

-deprivation

you broke my spirit so I broke your heart

SIFTING

you broke
and I froze

now you are in pieces
& I am loveless

which is worse:
    to cut yourself off from feeling anything
    or to hurt with everything you have?

-breakup

I may have forgiven you
For what you stole from me
But I have not forgotten –

I know this because
When I see you walking towards me
My muscles tense
My heart steels
My eyes are ice

To you
I may appear fine
Unaffected even
Civil words may escape my lips
But I cannot promise
Any of them
Are true

SIFTING

Tell me about the relationship you want:

is it of freedom
or restriction?

does it elevate
or destroy confidences?

does it make everything magical
or everything difficult?

does it sing praises
or voice doubts?

does it simmer with sensuality
or turn cold
with the passing of time?

you cast the longest shadow on my life
but now I'm all sunlight

SIFTING

I don't need more closure
Or somebody else
I think that it's time
I come home to myself

ON MY OWN

He sheltered me from them
Until I felt unsafe;
Caged
And I ran back home.
Then they sheltered me from him
Until I realized
That what I really needed
Was to learn how to shelter
Myself

-codependent

SIFTING

when you're shining like diamonds
who needs one on your finger?

-single

I want to live somewhere
That offers deep permission
To breathe
To just
Be

I want my own place
An oasis
A nest

I want to live and create
Freely
Abundantly
With gratitude

I want to be seen and loved
For my soul
For my complexities
For my depth

I want to relax completely
Into this moment
Into this rich life

-desires

STUDIO

By choosing this apartment
I choose myself
I choose a room of my own
Space to unravel
Safety for my tender heart
I have set my boundaries
Clearly
And he doesn't have to accept them
For them to be valid, happening, & true

I walk into my apartment, lock the door behind me
and the whole world is quiet

Exhale –

I melt into the soft ripples of *soulitude* that hold me
like an ocean
Buoyant and rhythmic and healing and safe

I delight in my surroundings and become one with
them as shoulders relax and jaw softens, fully
absorbed in the fullness of life untainted by external
forces

My mind inhales a rhythm and a hum that fills me
and floats me back to myself
With electric calm coursing through my veins I melt
into the soft familiar frequency
Of abundance
Unashamed and unrestricted
Empty of the need to prove myself or explain myself
or even define myself

I ride the waves of my whims, doing only what
feels natural, gliding like a pinball content in the
four walls of its machine, giddy in the ease and
weightlessness I feel in my zone

SIFTING

Free—
        To make mistakes
            And messes
Free—
        To take alternate routes
            And live life on my own terms
        Without another soul telling me otherwise;
        Threatening the clarity of my instincts
            by suggesting a different melody
            a different outfit
            a different parking spot
            a different truth

I decide again that I am the paintbrush and life is the
    canvas
My strokes need not be perfect or even make sense;
    and
The ONLY person allowed
        To refine my actions
        Or suggest an alternate route
Is ME,
        And because I strive to treat myself like a dear
            friend
        With the utmost kindness and non-judgment
        With thoughtfulness and radical care
        There is no friction.
I am the universe. The universe is me. I belong to the
    moment. I belong.

If I allow myself to
Soften back into the things I love—
To be as sensitive as I was made to be—
To welcome joy again—

If I give myself permission
To just breathe
And move
And indulge in my senses
And quiet down
And disarm
And write
And just be

What would that look like?

-recovery mode

SIFTING

I'm worried that
whomever I become
intimate with
will
minimize &
invalidate
my most vulnerable feelings
when I express them—

Unable to meet me in
the darkest corners
of my being

Unable to simply
bear witness
to the truth of who I am

-loneliness forecast

how many times
will I have to tell myself
"I'm OK now"
before the sun rises on its own
without me pulling it
from the ground

SIFTING

I used to be the softest thing
I am a fortress now

I'll never judge a soul again
Now that I know
What rock bottom is

SIFTING

I'm either running from love
Or drowning in it

-finding boundaries

How can I let
Another person
Be my home . . . my world
When I have spent
So long
Building my own?

-interior life

SIFTING

I want a man who won't leave me alone
Except when I tell him it's time to go home

"You deserve someone
who is going to embrace
your creativity +
elevate your sense of self"

-advice from a wise friend

SIFTING

I want to learn
how to love deeply
+ detach well

so that I can remain in relationship
instead of running when the flood rushes in

-interdependence

I'm so afraid to step back into
The wild unknown
With all of its unanswered questions
And anxieties
Its feelings that course like rivers
Through bodies with
Shaky legs trying to stand—
Full of tender hopes and dreams
Waiting with fidgety fingers for their names to be called
Longing to be assigned a place in the world
A purpose, abundant and clear

REBOUND SEASON

"You can't mess up
What's meant to be"

-dating mantra

SIFTING

tall, dark and wrong for me
one look – weak at the knees
music when you speak to me
say anything
say anything

tell me with your body
the things you're too scared
to put into words

SIFTING

you take me to the edge of all good things
then leave my high hopes lingering

-almost love

you planted kisses like flowers on my head
I never minded you messing up my bed

SIFTING

you
lit a candle
in every room for me
now I live
by the light of your memory

-old flame

I can still hear the sound of
The front garden gate
Shutting behind me
Sealing our fate

It never mattered
How long or how late
You'd open the door
We'd fall back in place

Eyes full of stars 'til the next morning came
And there wasn't a single word left to say

SIFTING

you want to live fast and loud
but I hear symphonies in silence

-opposites attract

you lit a fire
freed my every desire
sent electricity through my veins

your kiss was a million love poems
steady and exciting
with every change of pressure
and position

how could I be anything
but grateful?

-ex

I spent an entire summer
Trying to see myself
Through your seafoam eyes
Only to wash up
A stranger
In the fall

I'd choose you every time
If it was up to my body

SIFTING

Are we safe from the flames yet?
Took a sip and got wasted again
Holy grail to cold pavement
And the price of this magic
Is madness

-physical love

we like to move like
oil and water
someone's son
someone's daughter
always on the run

we like to hide and
blame each other
too afraid
to drop our armor
and soften into love

SIFTING

good chemistry
bad experiment

-me + you

MEGHAN SALETTA

your heart is an ocean
your love – a potion
but not for me

SIFTING

love hurts the most
when it's an almost

there's a bigger
full-bodied
YES
out there

-don't settle

CLOSURE

it broke me
when I reached out
2 years later
and you told me
you were fine
& hoped that I was too

the man I left
was in pieces—
and look at you now:
you'd made yourself whole again without me

now it was my turn
to break & rebuild

-grief

SIFTING

open wounds
deepest fears
you held me through
those tender years

I think the reason I loved being with you
Is because we got to be children
    Free of responsibility
    Full of magic
    Oblivious to reality

-first love

I did not know
how to cope
when the footprints ahead of us
disappeared
& it was only me and you

-trailblazers

//

there was a point at which
practicality and predictability
became more important
than passion and spaciousness and love

-the dying

//

we were a mountaintop love
but we died in the valley

-young

if I remember
>how you loved me tenderly
>how you melted my walls
>>and held me in perfect weakness
then I will blind myself to the ways
I became
>>caged and isolated
>>judged and small
>>a prisoner of your perceptions
>>voiceless in the name of loyalty & love

-unhealthy

SIFTING

maybe we weren't selfish
maybe we weren't wrong
maybe we were just young

find a lover
who doesn't make you choose
between who you are
and who you are
to them

find a lover who is strong on their own
who lifts you up and makes you laugh
who protects your freedom
+ celebrates your independent nature

find a lover
who
loves you wild

WISDOM + ENCOURAGEMENT

the path
to freedom
begins
upon realizing
that you are wholly responsible
for yourself

SIFTING

whatever makes your soul sing
is probably the right thing

Live every day
Wide open
Like a flower
With your face
To the sun

-mantra for thriving

SIFTING

your energy
your patience
your cadence
is a gift

-the way you make others feel

there are certain things in life
we *have* to do
the rest I'd like to play
by ear

-freedom

SIFTING

thoughts are like clouds
drifting across the skies
of your brain

watch them

    notice their unique form

name them

appreciate them or ignore them

let them pass...
in peace

    they always will

do not attach yourself to their contents

far too wispy to be
reliable

    let them pass

cling only to your fundamental state

which is calm
which is peace
which is unshakeable joy

Your time will come.
It will.

And all those sleepless nights
Breathing through tight muscles
And a storm of swirling emotions
Will fall away and soften and release

Bad decisions
Bad boyfriends
Bad days
Were all just stepping stones
Somewhere on the path to

h e r e

Where knowing will wash over you like
A blanket of peace

Trust the timing of your life
It's yours
You can't miss it.

Don't be afraid to let people in. There is nothing more beautiful or liberating than being loved for exactly who you are. Let people see you at your most vulnerable, even on the days and in the moments that you don't feel worthy of tenderness. You are. Let love nourish, heal and help you. Do not feel guilty or ashamed for receiving help from others - you know you would do the same for them again and again and again.

it's not about saying the right thing
it's about simply being there
picking up the phone
sitting at the edge of the bed
looking into the eyes of a person
who is hurting
and saying with mere presence
I am here
I see you
I acknowledge your pain
You are not alone

-how to help

SIFTING

I'm not in this alone
You're not in this alone
We're not in this alone

honor your insides
live from within
radiate your truth
& your light
do not abandon it
for any earthly thing
or person

SIFTING

take care of your spirit –
it is the spark
that lights
everything else

to savor each moment
like a bite of decadent chocolate cake
make your own rules
and set your own pace
is to have your life
and enjoy it, too

movement is medicine
sleep is medicine
gratitude is medicine
deep breaths are medicine
authentic connection is medicine
creating is medicine
total acceptance of self
is medicine

-Soul RX

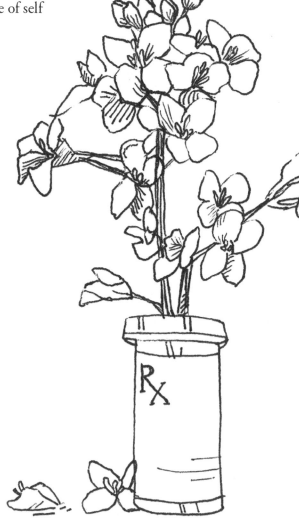

unexpressed emotions:
don't swallow them.
set them on the table
try if you are able
to name them in the light

for as long as we are honest
all will be alright

SIFTING

moods are like storms
they're just passing through

If praise is your drug
A time will come
When it is no longer enough
To measure your worth
By the applause of others

I hope
Instead of spiraling downwards
You give yourself permission
To stop reaching for prizes
That were never meant for you

I hope instead
You sit under the willow tree
And watch the water
Until the ripples remind you
That stillness
Is enough

SIFTING

sometimes
the hardest thing
we are called to do
is to sit still
and weather whatever comes our way
without running

-root

There must be power
In waiting
In standing still and letting
The waves crash &
A thousand different weather patterns
Pass overhead
All while keeping both feet
Firmly planted in the sand
Seeking nothing
But
The whispers within

SIFTING

pain won't kill you
but armor might

//

the vulnerable
always win
because even when we are belittled
or misunderstood
or brushed off –
we are standing in truth
and that
is power

there are a lot of kinds
of freedom
in this life

but none greater than the freedom
to be fully and authentically yourself

SIFTING

You are loved
As you are
Without trophies
Or gold stars

Figure out who you are
& what you believe
Write it down
When the time is right: share it
Then: stand behind it
Defend it
Don't let others change your narrative
It's *your* narrative

SIFTING

I love the idea that
none of us has a fixed identity
that we are so much more free + versatile
than we think we're allowed to be

-embrace your parts

please
never clip your own wings
to make someone else
feel more comfortable

learn how to disappoint people
& survive that moment

-boundaries

please
go easy on yourself
so you can go easy on me
and we can go easy through this life

-how you treat yourself is how you treat others

SIFTING

You are infinitely beautiful and full of wondrous light

May you welcome movement

In your mind
In your body
In your dreams & desires

May you be a vibrant vessel
Full of spaciousness and light
Ready to receive all that is for you

SIFTING

You owe no one your urgency
To protect their comfort
You do not have to answer right this moment
You can say,
Let me get back to you
I need some time to think about it
I'm not sure yet
Or, simply:
No.

The world praises productivity
I praise intention
The world praises perfection
I praise progress
The world praises hustle
I praise mindfulness
The world praises success
I praise happiness

-v a l u e s

SIFTING

listen to the whispers of your heart
and don't run
right when the plot gets good

MEGHAN SALETTA

don't delay JOY

SIFTING

if you live to please others
you will become a dry
shriveled up version of yourself
devoid of the lush beauty
that used to decorate your soul

hold on dearly
to your pieces
love and appreciate them
as you would another's

gather them around you
like a warm blanket
& bask in the coziness
of your wholeness

Treat every day like a treasure
Because none of this
Lasts forever

SIFTING

Free her
She who wants to run
And jump
And wear warm sunlight on her face
Who wants to laugh loudly
Dream boldly
Dance from her limitless soul

Free her—

She who is imprisoned by a fear-based culture
Sitting in a cell
Fingers turning white gripping iron bars she never
  asked for
Head hung low
Wondering if you will ever notice
How alone she feels
How trapped, bored + tired

Free her—

She who is a whisper born a ROAR
Who is unmoved by small talk & "what do you do for
  work?"
& people who exist only to keep everyone around
  them comfortable

FREE her—

She who longs to travel
And explore
And fail and learn
And fly
And follow her bliss
Without fear of judgment from those who only see life
    one way

She who longs to wear authenticity like a blanket
& never take it off
even when the heat of loneliness and rejection
    threaten to burn her up

FREE HER—

She who has been hurt by others but still belongs to
    herself
Who has learned from experience
And takes responsibility for this
ONE wild adventure of a life
She who is ready

Free. Her.
So she can finally be whole

SIFTING

The truth is, you don't have to try. Your worthiness is inherent. But when you do try, my suggestion is this: try authentically. Try in the direction of your dreams. Try in alignment with your values. Don't fight against your soul's unique current. Go with it. And see where it carries you.

No matter where you are, where you work, who you're with or what you are trying to pursue, you will find eventually that there is a **you** that is unchanging. No matter how many masks you wear or pages you turn, there is a part of you that can't be altered. The more you go out of your comfort zone and try new things, the more you interact with people who are different from yourself, the more you travel, the deeper you love and the more times you fail, the more in touch you become with this inner **essence** that just *is*. That's your soul. That's divine breath in you. The part of you that needs nothing except simply to be.

I really regret
All that fun I had
Living in the moment...

-said no one ever

SIFTING

don't apologize
when it's not your fault
but do apologize
when it is

a soft heart
will serve you much better
than a steel one

you might sink
before you fly
countless ways
countless times
but you won't go anywhere
on the sidelines

SIFTING

sometimes
when you are the epicenter
of multiple truths
pulling you
in multiple directions

you will become exhausted
in the acknowledgement
that certainty is nowhere
to be found

certainty –
the balm that could certainly
cure this state of constant anxiety
we call life

but even certainty is a trap
because the moment you make up
your mind about how and what things are
is the moment life gets small
and uninteresting again

-stay flexible

sometimes you're flying high
sometimes you're breaking down
no matter the season
go easy on yourself

SIFTING

You are not a walking paycheck.

-reminder to men

shake off the shame
honor the stars
& be who you are

SIFTING

sometimes I think
the greatest gift
you can give the world
is your optimism

-bright spirits

I love (x)
But it's too
hard | uncomfortable | risky

-do it anyways

SIFTING

you are a constellation
don't become a single star
because someone said
your light was too bright for their eyes

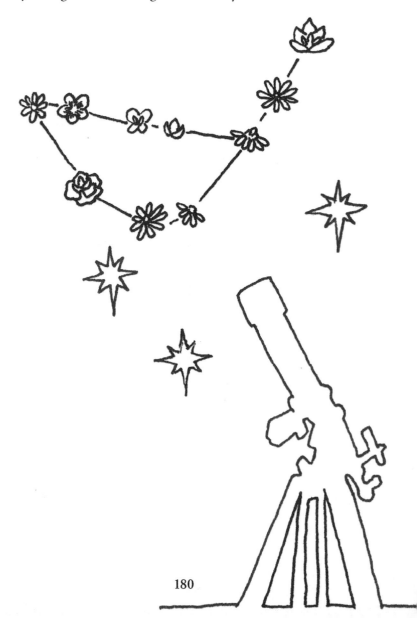

I hope one day
However unprepared
However painful
You wake up.

And see how beautiful the truth is
As it sparkles + burns
Like fire sweeping a field
Clearing everything in its wake
Until all that remains
Is peace

SIFTING

easy, child
you're doing fine
if there's love in your heart
and light in your eyes

CREATIVE LIFE

YOU MIGHT BE AN ARTIST

If you lay awake at night
Sinking
Deeper
Heavier
Into a starless darkness

If you feel it all
Too much
More than you want to
More than is reasonable
Or tolerable
Or sustainable
Then you might be
An artist

Get out of bed.
Make something of your sorrow
Fill the void with words and music and color
Offer it to the world

Suddenly
You will feel your soul breathe
A sigh of relief
You will feel

SIFTING

A lightness wash over you
That lasts the day

Savor it—
This is your reward
For turning mind
Into magic
This is how you get
To peace.

Keep on singing
When your lungs get tired
Keep on dreaming
With those open eyes
& I know the world can get heavy
& stars they don't always align
Oh but
Keep on singing
You were born to shine

-Darling's Lullaby

SIFTING

a child's only wish –
delight in me

    - an artist's only wish as well

I believe my simplest and most consistent calling in life is to admit to myself that I am a writer and write.

SIFTING

you become a writer
in the dark
in the stillness of a stuffy childhood bedroom
where unprocessed tensions hang in the air –
waiting for words like
friends to come over and play

you become a writer
to create a world that is safer
than the one that has failed to welcome
all of your colors and radiance
feelings and imagination
a hiding place
where no one can find you

you become a writer
because you have to

-a r t   i s   s u r v i v a l

My ego is so fragile
My dreams so insecure
That I cannot share my process
Without risking my footing

I do not speak of creating
Until I am done
Liberating
Whatever stirs me

You see a natural —
Because you don't see the work.
Early mornings unlocking
Melodies in my mind
Freeing words to dance on the page
While the coffee gets cold

Savoring
The safety of solitude
Where praise or rejection
Cannot yet touch me

And when courage comes
To sweep serenity away
To seize stubborn hands that cling to tender truths
To announce eagerly to the world,
'Look! An artist!'

SIFTING

all that's left
is a prayer in my throat
the s h a k y whisper of a hope
that
     you see her.

-imposter syndrome

poems are my roots
and songs are my wings

SIFTING

I've spent a lifetime alone in my room
Living in worlds you've never been to

If you're making them uncomfortable
You're doing something **brave**

SIFTING

"Thank you for sharing – that was so beautiful."
"I really felt that."
"I was moved to tears."
"I love your lyrics."
"That was really healing."

-ways to praise an artist

art is an ax
picking away
at the frozenness
inside of us

-melt

SIFTING

I wait in silence for my songs
They are a collection of feelings and experiences
I don't mention out loud
They are truth trapped inside of me
& it is my job to free them in the most beautiful way
I know how

MEGHAN SALETTA

it feels true to me
it feels complete to me
it has been healed
&
it does not define me

-rules for artistic exposure

SIFTING

my pen has started
to filter my thoughts
the way my mouth does
on trains
at parties

when the felt tip gets too close
to a crisp sheet of lined paper
it pauses and stutters,
are you sure?
ARE YOU SURE I should let the truth fall out?

Someone *will*
Reject this
Someone *will*
Disagree
Someone *will*
Unfollow

Can your heart bear to lose the masses in service to
The ones truly meant for you?

when I make my art about
impressing
instead of
expressing
the soul dies

SIFTING

go easy on the part of you
that is never satisfied
it is creating new life

every time I write a song I feel like I'm born again

SIFTING

If I didn't create
I would crumble
Or implode

The voices said:

You're too old
There's already someone else doing it
It's too tiring
It hurts too much
What's the point?
What if no one cares?
What if it leads nowhere?
What if you fail?

Courage spoke back:

Create anyway
Release anyway
Try anyway
Believe anyway

SIFTING

The road to success
Is paved with a LOT
Of NO's

Learn to say a silent "Fuck You" + keep walking

-rejection is redirection

it doesn't have to consume every waking moment of
   your day
or demand all of your energy + might

you don't have to parade it around
or scream it from the rooftops

all it has to be is a quiet, rooted, never-ceasing

"YES, I CAN"

   -how to stay the course

Fear says: *don't do it*
They'll judge you
You're too sensitive
It will hurt too much
It's not worth it
No one cares
You'll just be disappointed
The pain of exposure will be excruciating
You'll just have to top this next time
     And again, and again, and again...

-fear lies

no matter where you end up
in the human race of things

if you savor the journey
give thanks to the process
& wade in the wonder of it all

you will not for a single second
be disappointed

you answered
the call
to create

SIFTING

I am equally as uncomfortable
Receiving praise
As I am
Receiving no feedback at all

Both make me feel
Like I am not enough:

Praise, because it begs
"Do it again! – even better this time!"
Silence, because it asks,
"Have you even done anything at all?"

the fear that
if those closest to me
cannot fully understand me
do I even exist?

-belonging

SIFTING

every artist
needs an audience

one cannot exist
in an echo chamber

(it is our deepest desire
 to be lovingly witnessed)

An artist
Without an outlet
Is a ticking time bomb

SIFTING

I release
The younger version of me
That felt she had to
Practice her magic
In secret

Because the risk of
Being misunderstood
Was too painful to bear

What if I kept growing
So tall and true
And different
That you didn't recognize me
Could no longer understand me
And no longer loved me?

-evolve

SIFTING

I need to be challenged
Or else I will become
A victim of my ego
Unable to handle
New ideas
A thoughtful suggestion
Or criticism
Of any kind

I don't tell you much
About my pursuits
Because the moment I name them
My confidence vanishes

SIFTING

There are so many things society says I *should* be doing
But I don't do them

I lean into my rebellious nature like it is my only refuge
From the cold narrow pathways of the world

I am starving for belonging like everyone else
But I won't abandon myself for it

My nights might be lonely sometimes
But I hold tight to the dreams that seduce me
& keep me warm
When the outside world does not

What would happen if
I *really* believed in myself:
My ideas
My worthiness
My magic?

-the call

SIFTING

Old Belief: *I am a failure if I don't make a living from my art*

New Belief: *I will support myself financially while claiming the time/space to create + reach my dreams and goals*

m e l o d i e s come and go
but w o r d s have never left me

-a poet first

SIFTING

I become overwhelmed
When you weigh in on my dreams
Not because I don't trust you
Or value your opinion

Your ideas shimmer like sapphires
You know me deeply
Believe in me wholeheartedly
Want only the best for me
Forgive my flaws and
Hold me in highest regard

You have earned the right to hear my story
And I am so grateful you are a part of it

And yet
Your words feel like criticism
To defensive ears that did not
Summon more input
Your excitement an assignment
That leaves me shattered
And shut down
Because I don't believe in me
The way you believe in me
I don't forgive my flaws
The way you forgive my flaws—
I have to work at it.

In silence and on trains and in crowds
And on stage and alone and together
Everywhere my heart is beating
I have to work at it.

And so I envy you
When you get up from the breakfast table
Chair legs scraping shrilly across the hardwoods
Like they have for as long as we've gathered
You empty your red coffee cup in the sink
And go whistling forth into the day

And now
My plate is full
My heart is anxious
I have been reminded of how good it can be
And how far I have to go

Your innocent interest
Has reawakened my deepest joy and my deepest fears
Again
Just when I thought I might be rid of them—
The two forces that I work so hard to keep at a
comfortable distance
Carefully summoning only when I feel capable of
enduring their effects on me

SIFTING

Now
I am left with the hard work
Of remembering my potential
Wrestling self-doubt back into place
And bringing my dreams to life

-mother muse

My jaw and shoulders are tense
I'm having a hard time taking deep breaths
I had 2 margaritas too many last night and walked a
    mile home from the restaurant in existential tears
I'm wondering if I should contact multiple exes
If maybe it's not too late to go back in time and live there
on the sidelines of some soccer match
or sunk into his living room couch

I'm being extra protective of my time and energy
isolating myself from friends and family members
so nothing triggers me

It's the final stretch.

I'm exercising like a madwoman at the gym
weathering a storm of chatter in my mind
proud that I'm (mostly) standing in the eye
letting the colors swirl around me

I think about quitting my 9-5
and throwing in the towel on my dreams
all at the same time.
life feels chaotic and almost unmanageable
I'm praying that I don't get sick
or fuck this up
or crumble under the pressure and forget to believe in
    myself

so I can bring what I'm dying to bring to the world in
    it's entirely

I want this so badly.

I am my father's focus
& my mother's optimism—
I need both to succeed.

I remember why I don't live like this most of the time—
passion is unsustainable
uncomfortable
and slightly dangerous
but I wouldn't have it any other way

and I know that this is how I act when I am scared to
    death
moments before I step into the arena
& make some magic happen

Dear Creative Friends,

Sometimes – and if you happen to be sensitive + in tune with your feelings like me – a lot of the time, life will be uncomfortable.

You will face bursts of gnawing uncertainty, paralyzing fear, heavy doubt and dark nights of the soul.

Try not to run to 'fix' these feelings or numb them / wish them away. They are part of the total package of life + they are challenging you to open your sponge of a heart to the fullness of human emotion.

Let your pain be pain + your fear be fear. Acknowledge them, pat them on the head, get curious about them + don't worry about feeling these unpleasant things as deeply as you do. Thank God or the universe for giving you the type of heart + mind + psyche that is so much more colorful than the plain vanilla of a sunny sky all the time. Rejoice in the variety of thoughts in your heart + emotive landscapes + know that every high + low will pass and morph into something new.

When you feel terribly alone + none of your friends are calling and you're secretly glad they're not because what would you even have to say... take heart. I've been there.

When you feel down – like your brain doesn't quite match your surroundings or isn't doing its job or should be a few shades sunnier but feels stuck + blah... I've been there, too.

It's OK – probably most healthy even – to be sad + embrace sadness. Like winter, sometimes the landscape of your mind needs some 'down time' before flowers can bloom again. Trust your seasons, they are natural.

Also – maybe there are things going on in your life right now that are tender + hard + scary –and you've been trying not to let them 'affect' you but they just can't help themselves. Allow them to be & give yourself permission to grieve.

And if you end up spending a good chunk of this life NOT on Cloud 9 but rather processing + embracing the nuances and seasons that come with living life **fully awake** – then good for you. You are whole. You are human after all.

the magic is in the creative process
    not the applause
    not the lights
    not the fame
    not the money
it's the part in the dark
when its just you + the universe
    making something
    out of nothing

To My Parents -

Thank you for supporting me financially
    I never saw my imagination or creativity in the
    context of constraint

Thank you for not over-scheduling me
    This gave me the space and freedom to develop
    my inner world

Thank you for allowing me to shut myself in my room
    And spend hours alone becoming myself

Thank you for trusting me to make my own decisions
    Because of this I developed my own voice

Thank you for taking me in as an adult
    When I was broken or lost or in need of refuge

Thank you for your consistency and stability

Thank you for showing me how to soften

Thank you for showing me how to be strong

Love,
Your Daughter

INTROSPECTION
(IN THE LIGHT)

& I realized
I didn't have to be sunshine
All the time
For anybody
Anymore

28.

28 was the year I started feeling
more beautiful in less makeup
the year I made friends with the moment
and became fearless in the pursuit of fun

28 was the year I became my own guide
tore up the roadmap
veered from the trail of footprints
laid out for me
& started trusting my own rules

At 28,
I began to dream up a life for myself
at the intersection of
passion + intentionality
I woke up and realized
that this was called
Empowerment

I have a mind of my own
& I'll use it
To shape my e v e r y t h i n g

SIFTING

I am the authority on me

I have done my time
In the prison
Of other people's
Expectations

-free

SIFTING

There won't be a crash and burn
Because I will catch me
I have learned
How to sit in stillness
'Til the sunshine comes again
While a thousand different weather patterns
Pass overhead

I have built a home inside me
Where love and freedom reign
Where there is nothing to prove
And nothing to gain

[If you can sit with sadness
Honor madness
Hold onto gladness
Then you are doing OK]

if not this,
then something else
the greatest gift:
being yourself

SIFTING

I've been a free spirit since birth
I'll follow these whims to the ends of the earth

it's not that I lack willpower or responsibility
it's that I require joy

-adulting

SIFTING

I don't exist
To be
Who you need me to be

I exist
To be my freest
Most joyful
& loving
Self

I'm not strong because I never struggle
I'm strong because I *do* struggle
& then I rise

-again and again and again

SIFTING

I do not aspire to be a 'good' woman
Just a true one
Who knows the heartbeat
Of every cell in her body
Who is intimate with her pain
And indulgent in her desires
Who is patient with the storms of her mind
Who moves in gratitude
And sits in reverence
At the foot of life's limitless beauty
In a permanent exhale—
Wild + worthy
Without any need to prove herself

I love to walk and wander and unwind and drink in
    beauty and observe and be

I love peace and quiet and moments unfolding
    without a rigid plan

I like my life to pulse like poetry

-body-led days

SIFTING

I have learned that holding onto anything too tightly

People
Expectations
Outcomes

Just gets exhausting

I am made
Of stardust and imagination
The only thing I cannot be
Is caged

ACKNOWLEDGEMENTS

This book began as piles of "pearls" (scraps) scattered all over my bedroom floor. I'd like to thank my first reader, Ashley Trabue for encouraging me in the early stages.

To my illustrator Michelle Schultz – thank you for crafting the most emotive and beautiful images to accompany my words. You have become a true friend and source of inspiration throughout this process and I am grateful we found each other.

To my fiancé and partner, Mike – your steady encouragement and support while I brought this book to life is the stuff of dreams. From preparing delicious home-cooked meals to offering reassuring words to simply giving me the space to process and edit, your uplifting presence made it easy to stay the course. I couldn't ask for a lovelier support system than the one I've found in you.

To my parents – for giving me life and honoring my creativity since I first discovered my love of writing. Thank you for allowing me the space to dream; for supporting me financially when my pursuits were bigger than my paychecks, and for reminding me that I can trust myself.

To my brothers – you've shown up for me my whole life and seeing you in the audience gives me a kind of super-charged confidence boost that I find nowhere else. Thanks for being so supportive + so much FUN.

To all of the angels who keep my creative spirits high: Mom, Emily, Kim, Molly, Grace, – the list goes on. Your constant vote of confidence gives me reason to keep creating + sharing. & to my RONS – nearly 20 years strong: 'nuff said.

To my Kickstarter backers - this book would not have happened without you. Thank you immensely for your generosity in helping fund this dream of mine.

And to YOU – my reader – thank you for giving my words your time and attention. I hope they have nourished you in some way.

ABOUT THE AUTHOR

Meghan Saletta
is a poet and
singer/songwriter
dedicated to
expressing her raw
inner truth. She
lives in Chicago
with her fiancé,
Mike and her
lifelong journal
collection. This is her first book.

www.meghansaletta.com

Check out Meghan's music on Spotify &
stream "Sifting" – the companion album to this book.